D0356234

EACH TREE COULD HOLD A NOOSE OR A HOUSE

NINA PURO

New Issues Poetry & Prose

Editor	Nancy Eimers
Managing Editor	Kimberly Kolbe
Layout Editor	Danielle Isaiah
Assistant Editor	Samantha Deal

New Issues Poetry & Prose
The College of Arts and Sciences
Western Michigan University
Kalamazoo, MI 49008

First Edition, 2018.

ISBN-13   978-1-936970-54-4 (paperbound)

Library of Congress Cataloging-in-Publication Data:
Puro, Nina.
Each Tree Could Hold a Noose or a House/Nina Puro
Library of Congress Control Number   2018943184

Art Director	Nicholas Kuder
Designer	Ann Escamilla
Production Manager	Paul Sizer
	The Design Center, Frostic School of Art
	College of Fine Arts
	Western Michigan University
Printing	McNaughton & Gunn, Inc.

Each Tree
Could Hold
a Noose
or a House

Nina Puro

New Issues Press

WESTERN MICHIGAN UNIVERSITY

Contents

elegy with pilot light

Woman crying in a gallery

Shift Work

Acknowledgments

Portions of this manuscript appear in chapbooks from dancing girl press and Argos Books. My deep gratitude to the editors of the following publications who gave these poems their first homes, often in earlier forms:

90s Meg Ryan: "elegy with tripwire"
Argos Poetry Calendar: "elegy with five-finger discount on smallpox blanket"
Apogee: "Take Your Places, Ladies" and "elegy with credit check & one-legged pigeon"
Birdfeast: "Freelancing"
The Atlas Review: "Stop—You Were Never Gonna Get to Live on Their Farm / Plantation; When They Die Their Fascist Scion'll Take Over"
Big Lucks: "Woman crying in a gallery"
Bodega Magazine: "How to Live Where the Map's out of Scale"
Bone Bouquet: "elegy with rip tide"
The Brooklyn Rail: "Under Pressure" and "elegy with music box & warm deer blood"
Denver Quarterly: "Generation [   ]"
Devil's Lake: a section of "Bare Life"
ekphrasis: "Before the River Burned, but After It Ran Backwards"
Guernica: "Prescription"
H_NGM_M: "How to Ride into the Sunset"
Harpur Palate: a section of "Bare Life"
iO: "elegy with years my job was to not be seen & least favorite word"
The Journal: "Mile Markers Stitches, Power Lines Thread"
Jubilat: "100 Works in Mill Aluminum"
KIN: a section of "Bare Life""
Matter Monthly: "Shift Work"
The Nervous Breakdown: "Wrong Way"

No, Dear: "I Love My Country"
The Offing: "Mansion, Apartment, Shack, House" and "The Detritus Eaters"
PEN / America Poetry Series: "When she left,"
Powder Keg: "Self-Portrait with Backlit Jar Tourists Make Slow Circles Around" and "Service Industry"
Prelude: "How to Arrest Time by Crushing Rust to Powder"
Rhino Poetry: "Murmur in the Inventory"
Sink Review: "elegy with pep talk"
Sixth Finch: "Don't Speak Ill"
Sporklet: "Thicket of Pins"
Stonecutter: "elegy with burnt spoon & horse chestnuts"
Third Coast: "With Asbestos Exposed"
Thrush Poetry Journal: "Room Lit by a Bullet & a Photograph of a Pony"
Washington Square Review: "High Intensity Interval Training"
West Branch: "Key Table, Summer Hat," "Self-Portrait with Junk Bonds & Accordion," and "elegy with trillium & medical records"
Whiskey Island: "Self-Portrait with Genetic Mutation"
Witness: "Executive Action"
Zocalo: "Wheat Fields with Reaper & Unfinished Letter"

"Bare Life" takes its titles from Giorgio Agamben.

"Woman crying in a gallery" owes much to a 2015 protest of Carl Andre's Dia: Beacon retrospective in honor of Ana Mendieta. Titled "Crying: A Protest," the event was organized by Jennifer Tamayo and the No Wave Performance Task Force, among others.

"100 Works in Mill Aluminum" is titled after a Donald Judd piece housed at the Chinati Foundation in Marfa, Texas; "Murmur in the Inventory" borrows from an Erica Lewis title.

For friends whose invaluable feedback, patience, and encouragement helped shape this manuscript: Chase Berggrun, Cindy Cruz, Natalie Eilbert, Krystal Languell, Allyson Paty, Alexis Pope, Emily Skillings, and Wendy Xu.

Eternal gratitude to more people than I can name, including Ari Banias, Rijard Bergeron, Ahmad Bilal, Emily Brandt, Anne Boyer, Ana Božičević, Chia-Lun Chang, Iris Cushing, Oscar Cuevas, Joey de Jesus, Rebecca Fishow, Karolyn Gehrig, Bhanu Kapil, Mike Lala, Rachel Levitsky, Carrie Lorig, Louise Mathias, Saretta Morgan, Ali Power, Danniel Schoonebeek, Aime Sherman, Sara Jane Stoner.

To my family, both bio and chosen—particularly the Belladonna* Collaborative.

To all at New Issues, particularly Kim Kolbe, Nancy Eimers, Danielle Isaiah and David Rivard.

For space, time, and money: the MacDowell Colony; Eileen Myles and the community of Marfa, Texas, particularly Tim Johnson and Ryan Paradiso; Mellow Pages Library; the Constance Saltonstall Foundation; the Helene Wurlitzer Foundation; the Barbara Deming Fund; and all at the Syracuse University Creative Writing Program.

Before the River Burned, but After It Ran Backwards

Before the River Burned, but After It Ran Backwards

If they ask after my
even teeth
with enough scum.
the cornfield from above is
orchard, fingers
air. I'm swooping
gonna land
a horse, a penny
of my tongue.
I'm good at. I'm long
I know where
Born with cornsilk
teeth. Our kind's
real quite yet. I hold
under the lake &
of a smoke plume & hold
my tongue. If you question
behind the jacarandas
that means
there's no side
a draft. That means
your dad's lake. Each second
ringing right before
between my teeth all day
in the thicket with
My friend
lamplight through
of snow. My friend

whereabouts you tell them
can grow wings
It's cruel, isn't it? How
city, graveyard,
holding mum
over y'all & not
for a bit,
gumming the root
There's not much
done trying.
the pollen's blown.
between chipped
not kilt off for
my fear's head
hold the hand
bees under
whether you'll stop over
in that thicket tonight,
you will. That means
door that don't have
there's no way out of
a phone stops
someone picks it up. I lie
& later lie
my friend.
she spills
her hands like a photo
she has nine

9

fingers and three　　　theories for how

the world will end.　　　The one where *girls*

are swimming under　　　the ice & at the same time

standing on it to pour pitchers　　　of milk for tables thick

with white men. There's　　　the one *where we put*

the horses　　　down each Christmas behind

that burned-out　　　strip mall, & every day's

Christmas.　　　The one that's simple:

there's a cave at the center　　　of the globe with a butter-knife

stuck in the root　　　of stalactite teeth,

an empty stomach　　　a fist

fooling itself full　　　with fingers

& nobody makes　　　promises

no more. When they die　　　that's it. They've

loved. We　　　love. *That one's my favorite.*

That's the story　　　I follow home.

Easy Ways to Survive between Raids

Wrong Way

the last patients
leave through a curtain
of marigolds. the
hospital closes like
an eye

prairie boys
in john deere hats
& burger king crowns
run through
all our meadows

the sparrows in her tattoo
forever fly towards me
yet the bows never untie
the wind under the banner
never changes

i have this oiled black
wick in me & some
questions for our
darkness night refuses
to answer

i don't know how many
times i almost-died as a kid
but i know most faces
i loved i've spat at through
shatterproof glass

i'm around

Prescription

If afraid, cured leather & wood-smoke. If forgotten,
sassafras & hominy. If remembered,

bright blue hook. If bereft, lamb
sizzling. If rupture, obsidian &
chickweed. If suture, sleep curled around

a pine tree. If surge, puddle of milk. If shadow,
puddle of gasoline. If gender, shadow hurtling
overhead. If gender, dream in a language

you don't know. If gender, swim
parallel to shore. If morning, sunspots

& black pepper. If mourning, black
spot on a lung. If harvest, blood
sport & blood work.

If language, cracked
branches. If ghost, funeral suit worn
thin at the knees. If rainstorm, core

of candle. If closeness, death wish & warm
dram. If hunger, human. If starving, suture

& nuzzle. If caught out, folly
and muzzle. If walk, decade of
tiny crosshatches. If ruby glass, pick out

the stitches with your teeth.
If itch, reorganize the sky.
If itch, dropped stitch & chipped

saucer. If blackout, cinnabar
& fallout shelter. If walk, keep walking.

How to Ride into the Sunset

Tempe, 1999

I don't know how to hold this
without arms I mean
I know I have arms I don't know
what I mean our living
room a desert even
snakes have arms here
lizards know rough deep things
we forgot we are swimming
like thieves through tunnels
through hanks of dirty glitter
our speed monitored by aircraft
we are toilet trained
by and large we have free
lighters and rotisserie chicken
it tastes like snakes
you taste like the snow
this dry dirt will never know if
we started a fire the snow
would melt in a circle
sit down and get uncomfortable
there is no talking stick in genocide
I couldn't see the right
distance but I wrapped
scarves around it walked
into a new body nothing
is that hard only diamonds can cut
diamonds we're not that fancy our pH glistens

white skin in security cameras
a sunset makes no noise
there's water somewhere
outside us we are mostly
murky water inside
the all night
pharmacy where we blue
lights spilled into the yellow
from the drivethru
across the street where we
Nebraskaed our fear to a
sparkle we could swim through
found a kind of heaven laced
with napalm inside
that one kid's locked garage.

Self-Portrait with Backlit Jar Tourists Make Slow Circles Around

Dream your body
a yellow kitchen & fill it

with a family laughing,
a family coughing.

Dream your body the empty
house next door.

Wake to find your body the roots
clogging their pipes,

their burned-out block, the match
that started the tongues belling out, out and

out, the soldier that struck it, the church-bell,
the milk-teeth of the general

rotting in a jar.

How to Arrest Time by Crushing Rust to Powder

All winter the girls roll tobacco leaves to smoke,
curl in the cab of the pickup
to look for the moon in the dimple of a bottle.
Their breath glazes the panes, steams into cotton
to match what spills with the springs from the ripped seat.
The girls' voices the fall of a handful of nickels.
The slurring of choices into a singularity:
the baggie lying on a glazed blue saucer's chipped edge.

A hank of hair's yanked back, a throat exposed,
etc. In the trailer, the kitchen light stays on all night.

They don't know yet how sick they are
or how far "*better*" will be: the fall of struts,
the sulfured flare to tinder of such fine white bones,
how fast & quiet a grease fire blooms. The tallest

girl sets bowls of water outside: to catch what
stars there are. To let freeze over, to melt
come morning, to drink when chills set in.

As spring edges its palm in, the girls blacken
the edges of their eyes to match
the black of maples against snow:
to practice marking their own lintels
with something more expensive than blood. Frozen

tire-tracks soften to mud; tracks
in their arms harden. They learn
to pay rent by turning their eyes to fists
grasping in the VFW parking lot. Their skins turn
to minnow scales, slip past the sheriff's cruiser
while takeout styrofoam ghosts across the yard.

Thicket of Pins

The milk they fed you on long
soured, but you give
it. Given name *Blackberry*
Bramble, your given name
Queen of Sorrow. We are all
so thirsty in the village
of what we once believed. Don't
you know where to hang
god's eye, Blueeyes? Don't
you know language is useless? That I
stitched the blanket? That goodbye
lasted a decade? Goodbye
each room's still flooded
to their chandeliers. Goodbye
fish swim slow circles between
the chair-rungs. Goodbye
they know a language we don't. I can't
name the marled color of the fishes'
eyes or how they match the crystal
tumblers broken & always
full now—or how the glasses
match the warm cups that suck
poison from your back in a
backroom where the radiator
hisses but the curtain's filled
& emptied & filled with cold
from the cracked
window. Your spine
an open door. I'm not sure
now if memory is one
air & history the other or we're

the blade where they
meet. I thought we'd be more
than air swallowed or said, motes
& glass insulators for miles lined
on sills. Goodbyed the one sill
where the jasmine tendrilled out &
out & browned into a broken
umbrella. I've this to give: I'll go back over
the goldgrass hill to where the little house
was kerosened, walk in the split
house still smoldering. I'll
go back glad. Put the body in bed.

With Asbestos Exposed

We scramble as beetles silvered by moonlight.
      The abandoned house across the street's open when
the barroom isn't. Some nights, we sit in a circle
      in what must've been the living room. Heights in pencil
ladder up a blackened doorjamb.
      I pick your singed hairs out of piles
of metal & mercury pooled
      on the ground. The burned-out ceiling
is a ribcage. Our skins shades
      of char. We flinch from paper, lie
on cooled planks & mark patterns on the floor
      boards, save cigarette butts to fix in rows, humming.
Call us *marked by some invisible sign;*
      call us *thieves,* call us *done for.* I won't call & I want the future
to stop. Or go. I want to crouch inside scarred places
      & understand what must have been the blade,
& why. I don't understand why copper
      is so valuable—or the past. The walls graffitied
to a petroglyphed muddle I can only squint at. We can't remember
      languages we've tromped on or where the locks are
but we've keys. Our country's beautiful and wants us
      dead in the most casual way. Mens' voices shudder
window glass—thin as the skin on water
      at the top, thick as bargain china at the bottom.
Knives in the middle. I beat time
      with my hands on the sill.

Freelancing

I don't know what she wanted
    that summer we stitched our dresses
        into ourselves but I know

I kept looping needles into my skin and smiling
    wide at a camera, sweating
        in the small of my back. Each stitch

made me feel a little better,
    or so I told the mirror. Each ground
        a tiny contusion in the sky; a hum

in my backteeth. A footstep,
    a new black spot on a lung.
        I know I got jacked three times

and was only drunk one of them.
    I don't remember the faces of the women
        I slept with or the men who robbed me.

I know each hour clicking over was a thin
    needle of gin. One time a notebook burned. I dreamed
        it first. That means I lit it. Once I waved my hand

and combed the clouds straight as Venetian blinds
    just so the slats would fall pretty
        on her torso as she posed

for a selfie. Good days started
    with an idea, then continued with twisting it
        until it snapped in two.

Wheat Fields with Reaper & Unfinished Letter

Our data still glimmers from their cave
in the mountain, but dark comes earlier up here

between big shoulders. The men want our secrets to crack
as gulls eat clams: by dropping them from high.

The puppetmaster holds court. Jealous peasants'
faces float dour above cunning little lights. The believers try

joining. Our shadows graze on the porch, headlights
passing headlights. No, flashlights on gravestones.

No, topography cross-sectioned, & the man's finger
pointing to the rift, & the radiumed sliver where the femur snapped.

I should write to you more. I'm sorry. Each evening,
evening thunders in: trailing narcissus, direct-to-sepia.

The paper says the shootings will increase, like the famines,
as our water goes. A grand magician's favorite tiger died.

Ours is a century contaminated on either side
like a weekend. Bees love the pears, which are ornamental,

like me. A woman says *I'm so glad we finally got to reconnect.*
A famous man replies *Great to meet you.* In our group photos

I can't unsee who would've been shackled. Last century I molded
my apology to the shape of my body then stepped out

of my body. The new war leaks its music into
the meadow. I'm trying to drink more water.

The big lion's paw on my chest is mud-caked,
cracked. Once you said *there, there,*

there was *a lake in you the size of a mirror.* I didn't dare
ask how big the mirror was. That was long ago. Before

I could point to where I was done for.

Bare Life

I am not sure if what I wanted for myself, once, was a witness. To
what happened. To naming what happened. No way to describe. The
tyranny of language cannot. To have cut how many cities down,
bodies back, plastic rings from soda cans & balconies & receipts. A
sky particulate: engraved with fine tracings, latticework or ironwork.
A buzzing in the room. I didn't know where from. Light-specks
floated from our feet, as if we were an inauspicious constellation. As if
radioactive.

There is the past & there is the past. There is the sound of metal in
wind—off-kilter, tonight. A boat with no ocean close. As if it knows
something in the low tones, as if warning us in the high. If the ghosts
are back. In the close-packed concrete room, I could see the whorls in
the girl's ears, the darkness that hung around her—unnamable
damage, something rent—& that was part of it: the witnessing. The
way her hair fell in dark wings along the mark the blade left. A gash
longer than the length of what we could understand—scale,
irrevocability.

During the hardest telling, she would revert to before-dialect. To
those gathered to listen, she was not so much a person as a
transmitter of history, a transistor radio between the ghosts & the
tribunal. They didn't want her well. Wasted. Figurative. I never saw
her again.

We are all part of a current, it is said, but perhaps it is dark. We
become agents to projects we didn't know existed. Become culpable.
Looking for truth as looking for bone splinters in a desert, one star in
a constellation. We get disappeared uselessly.

In the orchard of lost keys, the men tell us dead girls speak in unison or not at all. The men call arms impossible trees. Their arms careful rows of bruises. The dead girls miss us, but not much. More, they miss neon afghans. They do not miss the police or the war, but they worry for us. They miss eating fallen apples still sun-warm, miss drinking away their silver. They do not miss paperwork, but who would?

How much angularity in our laughter, abrasion in our mannerisms. A languid sort of decay, a torpor. Who disappears first. Truth was scratching the dry skin off knees. Truth was scratching the oily skin off a face. Each word a frozen trajectory—to fold death into life. To fold truth into the ghosts running in the halls.

They miss signing their name: that jolt of finality. They don't miss remembering. They knit sweaters of tangled mattress springs to keep the tree-roots warm, play the gutted refrigerator like a piano. Winters, they make necklaces from river-ice to hang from any limb lithe enough to hold them, tree or fragile girl. Mostly, they miss the ambulance before the ambulance came for them: the sound pulling up like a key stretched into music. The inverse of an ice cream truck. Something not final, not just yet.

How to describe a year of static, a decade in sheets? I stood for a long time by the window deciding: get dressed or jump. Eventually, I got dressed. The day churned on. Life's like that. We try to get dressed, and do not speak of our trial later, when we are dressed and have sailed grinning in. We wear the smartest clothes we can. Ghosts press themselves between the folds, into the corners of our mouths. Some ghosts are boats, some birds. Some ghosts are drunk and some are sober. Some ghosts are burning buildings. Some are frozen rivers. You could clasp the ragged elbow of a ghost and go almost anywhere, unblinking. You could decide to jump but not fall. All the people you've loved would come rushing at you, just like that. Their hands would knife right through you. You could stay standing by the window, ajar, gone agog. You could stay there forever.

Decode the frozen lawn & the lights on the frozen lawn for the men. The ghosts skating on the lawn. Faces lit from below (so as to be ghostly) telling ghost stories. In my left ear, a high tone flickers on & off. A current freezes in place. My road is nameless. Do not ask me to. Watch out for the lights in the woods. Drive toward the blue lights that flicker & away from the yellow ones that stay steady. Surely

not everything is dead out here, despite the tangles of piano wire in the dogwood. There are codes invented daily that make machines do things. These codes are much less complicated than the codes in each cell. There are blue stars & there are yellow stars. Count them. Count until your counting runs out of room.

Mile Markers Stitches, Power Lines Thread

The train comes slow. Your face a glaring lamp
     clicking off. Each ticket blank: eyes open underwater.
         You crawl toward winter: deep blue, steam.

Leaf piles on leaf: there is propulsion in falling, a warmth in latent
     locust press. Here's the difference: matter over paydirt over
         deposits. We could cross the tracks—go down slow, make a trestle

of hands for feet, etc. I lie, waiting. I burned all your letters—they burned blue,
     cold. A hiss—wheat scythed. Even here, a ghost at the levers. Stars
         come: a gasp, a sheet thrown over our birdcage. Sometimes I glimpse

the bars, horizon-faint. *There.* That sky slackens, greased. One row
     of windows will feed the river; you'll end up on another side. Our dollars
         feed mountains, not broken-eyed backyards. Old tires, paint cans. A room's waiting

for us less than we're waiting for it. We started underground. We're not
     brave but we climbed, trusted the movement wouldn't split us. *I could stop*
         anytime, I tell myself. *Walk perpendicular to the tracks, start*

over. I won't, but every horizon will dissolve: accordion at the corners of our eyes then
     collapse, shear off as paper flung from a train: fractures of wind,
         dropseed, needle-grass. Rails hum long gray into our sleep. I want to believe

we'll click & teem with heat, glide polished. Now, though, you're cutting
     rails onto an etched mirror. It no longer reflects your face. That's the idea.
         What you know is not snow, as is said, but is numbing as ice or hours

of travel; akin to iron filings or powdered glass, but dearer. Snow against snow:
the starvelings shriveling: our want not light or train-steam but fleeting, numberless,
fist-fueled. Snow hides snow. You said we've a sister-life on another route

from ourselves & the train keeps moving. I lied: I still have your letters. White mens' faces
carried them to me. We were told about our power but in the end, it's too small
to misapply. We're steered through sheets of metal & magma,

every engine shaking—train, body, throat—burning
the last of the ash with the last match, burning all the fuel we have:
so we can feel we're going someplace good, somewhere fast.

How It Goes

Each ship after that first launch flung pollen across the map. No.
     Ships follow a logged course: radar & a figurehead & the finger
pointing to the crack in the earth's crust & in her leg on the x-ray; layers
     of calcium & migration, last lighthouse, bronze to iron:

river re-routed, Ionian to Dorian, waves guttering out, graves
     turned to paving stones, the road untraceable. No, the Catholic
church built around the holy Pueblo dirt, which was kept, which the sick
     still rub on the hurt bit. Which neighbors walked to Chimayo carrying

crosses the Good Friday I was born? Whose spirit stolen in the photo, which pic
     obsolescing into bugged code, which film's only reel melted celluloid
for the war? Which last speaker of what language died last night, which pattern
     lost when the factory burned, which note in a bottle, what did it want, which ship packed

in a bottle & tugged up with string, refugees in a hold, black box never found, black
     man gunned down by cops, which boy never stood ate what chickens never could walk?

Who never recovered, who died of sadness, unrecognized, died in the Middle
     Passage, whose work stolen, who never got caught? Which mayor snipped a ribbon,
which runner broke another, which door bricked over & bedroom sealed off, which
     dancer broke her ankle her first solo? Which fly trapped in amber, & miners

underground, & servant sweeping in volcano ash, & moth
     in margarine, & glitter in a snow-globe a boy shakes & shakes
& shakes? Who took the phone, the photo, the podium? Who traced the tree back? No,
     the family line daughtered out. Who took their last drink tonight, who their first hit,

what fingers snapped in place the wheel of the lighter hissing under the spoon? Who didn't cry
    at the funeral, who walked the bartender home, what cat waiting, which time
capsule never unburied behind the gym, above which who was first
    kissed, who first raped, which failed test exploded a beaker & burned the school,

what lighthouse burned out, which keeper had a bad fever that winter the gales blew
    so hard the supply boat couldn't reach it in time? Our loves burn towers towards our light.

When they arrive & take us it's our fault.

High Intensity Interval Training

They've hung a mirror above the hotel bed we'll

only sleep in. A heat mirage wavers in it
each time the train rattles by. We groom & gather sloughs,

drink from plastic cups wrapped in plastic. We look forward to going
back or we're here to look for someone gone. Heads grin
from three glowing boxes. They're searching for a girl. They multiply

into other heads. What we make in hotels is for how long
our bodies fill the bed before other perfumes
swim in. The way we fill & empty our
bodies changes over time— a slow spill. A break

backwards. Hands smuggle & muzzle through days.
What I spilled in & out of me I did in secret
yet in the confession there was a seizure—an ostensible cure
in searing it from me as a limb. When other people heard me
in the act, it was a horrifying impropriety.

I used to check into hotels with another girl for the breakfast buffet
& the toilet. We'd take turns going back & forth. Hands with light
shining through. We made a story, then took it away. Today, cops scroll through
the woods behind our hotel for the body of a girl. She was white
so they're making a fuss. In a thicket behind the third hill back, there's a hole
filled with parts of her but it'll take them three, four days.

For years, I thought I was only parts of a girl, but it wasn't that hard, I know,
I know because I walk around in my body. It wasn't hard. I can stare up
at my body feigning moans in the mirror & pray for a late checkout.
Hands two-stepping. Morning hands puffed loaves.
Blessed are those that today go missing & those that get found.

Blessed are those who tremble in doorways as mirrors, as screens, who
vomit up dinner, who walk across a bridge for no reason
other than that is a rope stretched between two needles
stuck into rocks holding a name. I said *hit me* & got paid.

I *no* & meant it. I said *we're good* & we weren't
but we built walls around the idea like a heat mirage. Dropped hints
the way helicopters disappear bodies into water. We can hit

each other with our hands like a hole in water where a body
slid in. We don't believe hands with nail-holes mean anything, so we can slot
our holes together. Because we're made of bodies we've absorbed, we can listen

to the back & forth of the air conditioner & the football players bashing each other
back & forth across a field on TV & the whistles back & forth in the hills
from men wearing blue hats & rubber gloves. Hands in the bells of flowers
& throats. Blessed are those "women" who wear their names
stitched over their chests who answer to men, those who don't work

under their name to answer to men, those who've changed. Blessed hands dropping
dollars into garters & those who catch snakes & bouquets & whose stomachs
drop like pennies into wells & those who drop the contents
of their stomachs into rivers. We can watch mens' flashlights sweep

back & forth on the wall above our figures blue & white
casting god. Like they've a divining rod of light that'll
illuminate a body swelling with water
or shrinking from air. There could be a doe
eating goldenrod in that girl's thicket. There could be beneath

our narrow bed a skeleton. There could be beneath the bedrock
a river, cold & sweet. An artery clogged: laced with arsenic, veined with gold.
My hands as clumps of stitches over veins. Hands sheened
with grease & sugar. Blessed is the falling empire. Blessed are those that run
through the woods, & those that hide in the woods, & those that sweep
food over scanners & into purses. Blessed those who peel back

the leaves over the face, those who drop time
-sheets into time-clocks, those who drop pennies into water
& over eyes. Blessed how much time I've spent digging
for a place to hide food. Hands as corkscrews for night.
Look how days roll over. A leaf browns or greens,

inverse processes back & forth with water. Clumps of bodies
weave on & off streets, streaming to work, streaming home, inverse
processes with time. Blessed is the coal that's left. Blessed those sinks
into barstools & TVs & bibles & sunsets

& beds. Our hands turn keys & steering wheels, turn into
kestrels & pickups & taproots. They clean bodies
& hotel rooms & pistols; grasp at rain, hammer out a new town,

set it alight. We get to swipe cards back & forth through machines
for dinner; in hotel mirrors to crush powder; to move our hands

through air against machines to refill them.

Room Lit by a Bullet & a Photograph of a Pony

What you did was a bullet, but I've drilled a hole through it
      & wear it around my neck. Sure you got a key-- I've seen it--
but it's a cheap one from the mall like every other crush has:
      plating wearing to brass. It don't open any locks.
In this Western, I ride bareback. Once I peed in the holy water &
      saw graves yawn open to flowers. When Daddy said drown kittens I did
& didn't cry. Today, I'm double-fisting anything I can &
      waiting for the river to become a cracked riverbed I can walk along
towards the scaffold I'm waiting to finish building. There's solitude
      in the long warm furrows of dirt in fields & in standing at the front
of a crowded train looking down the tunnel; a question
      about loneliness in the long barrels of pistols. (In a cold shovelful
of dirt hitting wood lined with fake satin, slow like how a balloon sinks
      slower in a dirty room.) An answer to the question in using favorite forks
& breaking favorite plates & in lightning bugs trapped in jars.
What you were: a photograph of a horse to someone
      who's never been on a horse. What I am: hordes of kids riding bareback
off cliffs with satin ribbons in their hair & the horses' manes,
      the satin trailing up to form a picture that shows where they're going next.
I had the same dream seventeen times in a row & I had it because I slept alone
      for once. Solitude in lipstick: a weapon by the bed brightening
as the cigarettes in the ashtray   & the fireflies nod
      out; solitude as the long black car arrives & the door clicks shut
with the sound of a phone cord being cut. (There's the end of
      solitude in the mirror on the ceiling. In the knock. In waking up
thirsty & drinking cold water.)   Falling back asleep
      to have the dream an eighteenth time, only this time all the faces are blurs
but I know who everyone is. (This time we're all dead.)
      Every person's voice is still ice clinking in a glass, but now
everything costs $5.99: almost a dollar more than I've got.

We depart, go new places— there's dust in our hair

      & not enough air in our lungs to blow the balloon back up.

I couldn't taste the metal in your key because of the glue on my tongue.

      If you chew gum while you dissect cadavers, it'll taste of formaldehyde.

I can taste my death in stamps & almonds (& if I spit the bitterness

      into the trashcan, I won't absorb it, but if I hold it on my tongue,

it turns sweet). I've been places downriver you aren't allowed

      to have shoelaces or listen to music or be alone. Where someone

sits in a chair & watches you sleep. When you sleep, sometimes you move

      through the dark. Sometimes the dark moves through you. Sometimes

the dark asks questions; sometimes it shoots.

Executive Action

If we were bunched then straightened
If the faultline was a crack
If the pointing looped inward
If her name dissolved as you said it
If smoke was coming out of her mouth
If her words were owned before spoken
If there were faces under the water
If the smoke formed faces
If translated from the []
If "welcomed" by heavy security
If heavy with salt
If in the bottom of the well
If in the pit of the stomach
If in the desert of the past tense
If my body shows up again
If the mouth of the river was dry
If this bridge called my back
If the bedsheet was a page
If the weft was a meadow
If parts of us die before we do
I want mine to be my selfish parts
By saying nothing what did I say
When my body was a harmonica
If information is a deceptively partial illumination
If our food is grown under the type of lights that give us headaches
If a dead person's kidneys filter N.'s blood
If she gets out of bed first I roll into the warm spot she made
If I rocked myself shut
If I want the feeling of sinking my teeth into frosting / crust / meat
If I wanted the feeling of sinking
If I wanted to feel

If I am falling into a headlong
If a shower of petals obscured her body
If a swarm of cursors covered her face
If the meat just falls away from the bone
If language is thick with hair and twigs
If her mouth honey and ginger
If her face changed under my fingers
If rain changed to snow
If the pans changed to drums
If the clock spun backwards
If my head folded into a swan
If our fruit changed to mush
If the bread rose
If the house sprouted wings
If the tunnel grew branches
If the branches grew dead ends
If the man changed into a woman
If the child turned into a mother
If the mother turned into a ghost
If every time was the last time
If you know there will be a next time
If no personal best
If the forecast was no
If she was a tall drink of no
If the year was a long no
If each bed was a page
If blank with no
If one scratches at the surface until one rips through it
If the arrow rushes into the future
If I speak with my fingers only
If I carry his water

Where dogs bark behind chainlink
If compulsory femininity seeps from the bag
Where the hole where the bathtub had been
If the hole her life curled into closed over
Where the hole for the trach tube
Where the site of infection
If her body is diagrammed in butcher's segments
If my body is threaded with roots
If these threads burrow across miles to you
If an open grave with all its magnets
If blown bulbs, *sicario*, your subway face
If the words blurred as she said them
If she flickered on and off
If the technocrats sneered behind frosted glass
If a new condo mushroomed up on each block
If her body was a rent check
If his body was an Uber
If hundreds of screens rocket under the river every six to ten minutes
If we pack ourselves tight enough to just barely never touch anyone
If she was packed tightly
If the day was loaded
If there was a kind of awe over it quivering
If who was under it all shaking
If all the tickets / receipts / bodies ribboned into confetti
If I thumb her face on a screen
If I brush a charged wire
If today as the gas tank light dings the third time I haven't spoken to anyone
If every door is a blue mouth
If there is no grief in this just the old body / year / world swallowing itself
If what's left has gone to grass and dirt
If a country on its knees

If a country with its back turned

If my body is a landscape

If his fridge light is the sun

If the borders were crossed

If the relentless present tense

How many died of hunger of gender

How many animal bodies were manufactured for my body to consume

If afternoon clicked into night easily as mah jong tiles across the kitchen table

If I was scattered with crumbs

If there was grease collected above the stove

If the food it spattered from became our muscles, our veins

If after someone moved the boxes from the loading dock to the shelf we moved
them into our rooms then placed the contents in our bodies and threw away
the container, what someones came before the loading dock?

If there was candle wax on the windowsill

If her name was an apple

If sand blew in ripples

If an idea was bubbling up

If I was a penny falling through water

If she were a pearl falling through soap

If the highway grew arcing loops in the city

If both our hair threaded the sink

If the drain is clogged with scraps

If the word in my mouth is a sin

If dust is mostly skin

If the shuddering planet my wake of plastic her wire hanger your passport

If we claim rings in the tree mark wars

If rings in the tree mark winters

If snow piled on snow accrues until it collapses under its weight

If loud noise can spur an avalanche

Who flinches when the doorbell rings
Who stiffens when touched
Who aches under florescence
When the green ray
If my body is a pitcher I fill and empty
How strong do we need to be
Where is the site of impact
What intervention is indicated
Can we try exhaling in tandem
How can I melt your shoulders down

How to Live Where the Map's out of Scale

I walk in the snow with my boots on backwards
so the police won't be able to follow me.

You should walk on the road with your boots on backwards
so the soldiers can't follow you.

You should sing something cheerful to the sound
of the glass that gets sunk in the soles.

When you hear the general has been shot,
you should run away from the square,

not toward. History's tide only
moves in one direction. We're in the undertow.

We're bottom feeders. The mud's soft.
I'll turn my face toward your light,

wait for the tide to part
or the roof to cave in. You should follow

water uphill & follow the name for each bone
you could break up your ankle, mumbled

in the old language, till you dance in,
safe. You should sink into bed

like a ship, sink
matches in candle-wax

to mark the dead, sink
needles in the sides to mark the hours.

Should stuff torn t-shirts in the bullet holes
that leak flickers through your door

but I don't want you to.
I want to find you.

When she left,

When she left,

was she a runaway, pregnant, kidnapped, hospitalized, a refugee, to
return or not, partially or fully; addled by chemicals that'd swarmed
in her body or that she'd shunted in; because of a boy or another girl
or her uncle; was she sent away, did she want to go; did someone pay
a price, a dowry or insurance premium or ticket—or if money also
went missing, how much; or was the payment waiting for her on the
other end; was she alone; did someone take her (is it someone she
knew), was a person or a place paid to take her; what'd they carry and
was it inside or outside their bodies—if outside the body what was
inside the parcel and how much did it cost; was it made of plastic or
metal or cloth, who carried the container and did it leave her side
and did someone search it for contraband— or were they waiting,
drumming fingers or clicking teeth to a bottle 'til they could knife
open the hidden seam like a neck; was something smuggled across a
border (was her body the container); was there a gun or a desert or a
dorm room, was there a secret room or compartment, a cell or hotel
or hospital room; was she given an address or key (which side of the
lock was she on); did the map make sense or was she trying to smell
where she was through a blindfold or was she following herself as a
moving dot on a screen, was there a river or highway or series of
fences to swim through, a horse or boat or pickup; did they apply,
did she apply; was it a form or contest or handshake or just
somewhere she fell, did she want to fall into something; was she told
what she'd do and was it true; was there a man at a desk or in a
basement or at a cafe or on a phone deciding, did the smoke of his
cigar blow in her face or did she never see his, just his signature or a
structure he'd opened with his voice; were there many rooms or just a
forest floor, was there a thicket to cut or a clearing that someone else
had made,

long ago; was there a shaft of sunlight and at what angle, was she told to sit in the clearing, then told something to gather or draw or think about or burn (did she burn sticks or bridges or cigarettes or papers); was she discussed at a wooden table and what was on and under the table, what were the people sitting around the table drinking; was her face veiled or disguised or made up, how much longer did her hair grow while she was gone and was that growth kept or sheared off and why; did her face appear in posters later, was it marked missing or with a crime and a number; or was it printed on a plastic ID card with a name; was the name hers, what power did it grant her; or was it just a photograph on a screen or paper someone kept in their pocket to rub under their thumb, whose thumb was it (was it hers years later); did she know someone took it, did she want them to; if on a screen did anyone access it or did it evaporate into millions of others, a sea of zeroes and ones; or was it projected onto a bigger screen; was the photograph how she was paid, if so did she ever see it and was she clothed in it or were the clothes or the room what was sold; did someone remove or add something to her, were her limbs arranged in the photograph or contorted and splayed, was one part that her body had grown or one part of her body missing—was this removal the evidence, the crime; or was this removal something that was done afterwards by someone else to erase some flawed part of her by clicking at light; was her face moving or talking, were the words her own; was it because she was missing or because of something else; if moving how grainy, was it from a surveillance camera or a phone or a video camera; would it be played again or duplicated onto other products made of cotton or plastic; would people paint her, would the paintings be any good; would they get tattoos of her, would she have hoped someone would; what would their letters say; would they follow her; would they have known it was her face where she came from; where'd she walk, did she learn to walk differently, faster or sexier or quieter or with shackles or heels or carrying cocktails (her own singly or a tray); or a child (her own or someone else's), to balance a hula hoop or a bundle on her head; would she learn to run for pleasure, or when someone called, or away from something crashing and panting behind her; was she buried in the forest or doing the digging and do we know where, was where a lie, is it marked, are there bones there still or were they removed; is someone sifting for the splinters—or does she look at the bones of her face in the glass in the morning and vow they're from someone she'll never go back to; will she come back or was she missing on purpose; what do they send her, what does she send them—if money, does one party ask for an amount or is as much as can be sent sent; how did she make it and is how she made it what she tells them; what currency is changed to what other, what do the faces on the bills see, what container were the bills collected in or were they sent by wires, whose voice was on the wire or was it just numbers; will they send for her, will she come back to visit or for good, back because she couldn't afford it or because she finally made enough to come back; will they have to pay a second time, to retrieve her or to give her to a man; will she be welcome (how will they tell her she is or is not); will her arrival be photographed, will she come back with the marked absence of someone or with someone else; will she come back to someone to wed (will she have met them); what will they make her to eat when she comes back, what did she eat in the other place and did she choose it and how—was it cooked in a microwave or vat or coal-burning oven, did she speak to who made it and did they speak the same language; what will she come back wearing and how did it change; how did she change, how did they change; do they miss her in the old place, are they still looking for her, how are they looking and how hard; do they think sometimes they see some hard-whittled angle of her some place she is not, was she spotted somewhere; how many places were there between, does she remember their names, are there places she'll never talk about; how often does she call to talk, to come back was she given a number to dial or did she know it by heart; was her body given a name or price or case number or ticket number (was she told it), did she choose it; how much of all this does she think she chose; did she want to go, did she find what she was looking for, was it the same as she thought it would be; what does she have to tell them about it, and how long is she staying?

elegy with pilot light

elegy with riptide

the conductor sways
the same way but we
can't see him in
his little booth.

we've paid
all the premiums
yet amber
bottles rattle
in the current.

we gum burnt
thumbs. turn
all the labels
in the cupboard
to face straight.

still the syntax
snags.

whatever's not defrosted
is in the phone wires
is fair game.

elegy with burnt spoon & horse chestnuts

thought
there were
tiny coyotes
in the walls.

could feel my lips
but they weren't attached.

lights harshing
the big rigs
sway in their wind.

snaggletooth girls
with takeout boxes.
little crucibles of heat.

we all have drowsy
recording devices.
chosen names &
families.
amplify the
dregs.

we are so clever.
we keep
coming.

shake my hand,
then count your fingers.

elegy with years my job was to not be seen & least favorite word

afternoon makes
a yellow noise
like wax. wax sutures.
wax teeth.

tongue stuck
at the root. pitiful
coldsore.

watch dad claw
air around the pawn shop
moon hammered tin

kinfolk swallow
hard when they
hear. keep
humming
almond wind & the
afternoon away.

decade I slunk
out of supermarkets
with full bags.
smiled at the guard.

my american
teeth
glint just
for me.

white thick
enough to swallow.
unpack that.

I'm tired.
I'm so tired.

Key Table, Summer Hat

We thought the site of earliest failure would be set with topaz
& hadn't already occurred. We'd know painters' names & if

the man standing over the woman had ravished or killed
her, & what each was. Thought we'd seen orchards but not

gallows, not yet. Not that both were in our yards, nor that we'd cut
both down cheap. Lives would curl in caves, stretch to tunnels, trap

door yawn the last second. We wouldn't watch glass thicken. Old
men, proud to clear plates, don't ask who washes. Their money's the

sleeper car in that dream we all rolled down gold hills & woke safe
& nobody'd become frayed gingham or died overnight & we got

why hair sparks in dry dark & men shoot their kids & women crawl
inside for good. We don't wake in another dream. I'd choose yellow

kitchen, Eames rocker; stride toward a useful anthropocene role:
a triage for the love blooming from me. The Board would hand it over.

elegy with trillium & medical records

swam through
a snowglobe with
drymouth
& a dirty t-shirt.

used to be
a click
when you hung up.

could greet folks
at the gate.

kept finding this skin
that wasn't mine
wrapped around
me. doctors kept
feeding it, drawing
charts of how
it grew.

I've watched how quick
a crabapple branch
can become a switch.

I love being here
& every fossil
fuel.

I've kept it so I
can't bring any more me
into this.

if we weren't
wax I'd remember
how to measure
smoke
kings burned a cigar
then weighed the ash

dozens of holiday weekends
spent speaking only to
the stove.

elegy with tripwire

dead mice behind
the stove, bellies curled
around poison
I scattered.

under the futon:
balloon dog, remote, dead
soldiers.

they've cordoned off
our block with coffeeshops
like they're making a moat.
we're the alligators.

drag up an invoice
for night
as if the projector
could silver our organs.

we drowsy
we slogans
slurred.

we icefoam over
the bridge's
struts.

what color the virus?
the brother's coat?

liver-light.
day like a fuse.
girl a paper bag
damp on the bottom.

elegy with credit check & one-legged pigeon

always end
at the beginning &
up at the Fulton mall
gold teeth gold
bow a little
fortress made of horsehair
& twist
ties a knot through
the afternoon's
neon where we sucked
a hurricane
down at D's
bar the windows &
the aneurism
not half
bad for a girl
clothed in smoke
& fishguts
I'm not sorry
for forgetting
even hollow
engines need
fuel but I'm
sorry for falling
asleep at the
wheel of what
we were gunning
towards

Generation [   ]

Smelling of river-water & razor-wire, we slouch to
cocktail hour, scowls bit bloody, slicked; bring cheap wine & what

can't be borne in canvas bags leaking gridlocked schedules. Toss us
crusts in gheed sourdough only, thx. Sure, the power bros said we
want

Seamless, but I'm here for revolution? Aware my attention span
predicates
its failure, public-me files the flagrant cynicism in obsolescing files.

Beloved our printing drawers, heirloom tonics; the winnowed rasp
of scythe. We've come to love each other, each dive bar

of our cell, bash lithe hips against the palace doorjamb, show
show off the bruise. Each sunset, silhouettes pose in said jamb, gel

today's death in a screen. We want the cat to speak. Naturally
this happens. We burn sins Tuesdays. Cue a brief humorous scuffle

with the fireplace, a .gif. Our dead dads, hair patience-thin, drive
our bad debt through their clear-cuts at this late hour, mapless.

elegy with linden tree three-years' dead still standing

noon like the wind
had a seam in it

men rolls of
concertina wire

house
born under
a bad star

women
a silk slip pooled
on hardwood warm

a year
borne
in a bad house

unter das
whose streets?
H&M

were it I meant enough
to be snipped
out of the photo

instead of
never in it

blown years
all those
cakes with
names on them

other girls
know how to
eat

in the movies the sidekick says
go on without me—don't look back!

I'm saying that
to all of you

elegy with pep talk

look I know I
was almost a goner

but there are fists
flying inside me.

each cups an ocean
or a switchblade.

take your pick.

elegy with parental mortality

some hours so perfect
I want to cry
to walk away.

please like a glowstick
or a fire hydrant,
not a winebottle.

I Love My Country

The jackdaw cries until sunrise. The people wait for a white man
    to tell them how to dress. I throw up breakfast. All morning, I pull out

my eyelashes and read Kristeva. My dying friend is rollerblading
    on Instagram. Cops shoot a rabid swan

and a 10-year-old. I am not waiting for love to come. I'm waiting for happy
    hour. Love is a transactional convolution. Breath is cheap. I'm not

waiting for my dad to die. Four poets sit on a black rock in the sun
    and talk about the moon. Asterisks accrue between my teeth.

Three men cut down a diseased elm. Their boots
    look sturdy. If I sell a poem, does anyone care? If a slowly dying

person finally dies, does anyone hear? I take my favorite panic
    to a reading. Each false note hums sweetly. In the dark, it holds hands

with my resistance. I eat the swan. I throw up diamonds. We're all breathing
    tree spit. My country is coming for me. Its pointy teeth shine.

elegy with five-finger discount on smallpox blanket

in the rectory's
back stairwell:
a key
made of glass. in
the woodshed:
a knife
wrapped
in a red bandanna

someone figured
out how
to silver-plate a river
hewn thin.

the same radio
station pumps
cumbia & gunshots
from: the dollar store the bakery
a passing truck.

all my friends
I don't trust
you but
I'm so glad
you exist.

come back
your tea's gone cold.

elegy with music box & warm deer blood

each invitation chloroform
trembling in ionized air
reject their strings
reject the duck I
cleaned of buckshot I
can't remember when the
attacks started
but they haven't
stopped something
will be sore tomorrow
I don't know what
but I'm doing it now
I bit the hands
that starved me
but they
were mine
just blow on the dice
& go
this thumb piano
ladders out a
spell to tether
safe the storm
each widow's on her back porch
drinking a warm beer
you know how
when numb fingers
get inside
they burn?
think of me
as that
feeling.

elegy with everything underneath my dad's sink

the house fragments
of bone
jimson weed
grows high
around
the water-pump
gone dry

scrap-paper
origami body
don't fold
right

good days stop shaking
long enough to salt
hours over my shoulder

pretty's a
door I can't open
down at the terminal
there's a girl with a
black eye waiting
for the boy
I could've been

I'm on my way
I text
I know

a girl's stuck
beneath the fryer

I'm on my way
I say
I know

Woman crying in a gallery

Woman crying in a gallery

is a rupture an artifact or just a wound?

        shadow that does not match the shape that made it

how much of grief is a performance to the dead?

        shadow sliding across a lawn

if the performance is only to the self, does a tree fall?

        rotten pears in a wooden bowl

how much of my starvation was a performance to the sky?

        vomit leaking from plastic bag

if the body is a house, was I burning it in protest?

        house as wine bottle filled with snow

can an action take place in stillness?

        mesh bag of clothes I couldn't sell

to what extent was I making myself an artifact?

        pallet of gently used winter clothing on a barge to Burma

to what extent was I a bad architect?

        pallet of H&M' s new spring line on a barge from Bangladesh

to what extent was I a lazy artist?

        people in a shipping container on a barge from China

to what extent did I invert the lie?

        people in line for bread or phones, sweating in rows of ellipticals

if at first I wanted to be small, then for 14 years couldn't get better,
was the disease always false?

        circle of women's bodies making snow angels

if we were not allowed to document it, did it occur?

        circle of thin white women's bodies eating

if starvation changes the brain, what else could have occurred &
would I remember more?

        voice on a tape in an archive

was it an effort to forget?

                                              Ana's body slamming into the deli
if starvation changes the brain, did I become fluent in a hidden language?
                                              to see snow, see her silhouette
if I got sick in order to leave, rather than the usual regression-into-childhood model, what was I
trying to escape?
                                              to see, try to unsee
was incessant weighing & measuring a comment on capitalism or a reiteration?
                          circle of thin white girls in hospital gowns begging to see their weights
did the revolving door in the Seagram Building blur to snowflakes or make me see better?
                          circle of thin white girls in kimonos taking photos with "warrior" makeup
when was the last time you got undressed & measured by a doctor or a man?
                                              silhouette filled with powder
on a warm February day, how far do you walk with your coat on without taking it off?
                                              silhouette drawn with white police chalk
how cold are your hands?
    circle of girls with sharpies on butcher paper, tracing how big they are vs. how big they feel
what color is the sky now?
                 in our separate showers, mornings, steam curled from our bones at the same angle
what about the color of the sky when you were born?
                                              white rock into a river
what coin from what country paid to stitch your mother up?
throwing up into the river quiet after snack
who wiped your mother's brow after? who didn't?
                                              phone ringing in an empty room
what coin over her eyes or under her tongue, later?
                                              whales in an ocean
what phone numbers have you memorized?

                                              murder sites on a map

what do you say into the disconnected phone in case the other person can hear?

public bathrooms & grocery stores on a map

so ok if my bulimia was stealing massive amounts of food & scheduled twelve-hour blowouts every 1-3 days, rather than frequent quickies while in & out of company, how do the lack of spontaneity & isolation play into what occurred, which is to say: did I protect the rest of my life & keep myself functional or did I make the rest of my life a waiting for that period?

I'm losing you I'm losing you I miss you

to what extent was the stealing poverty and to what extent adrenaline?

white bread crumbs on a kitchen table

to what extent gathering evidence I was a bad person?

white powder to gums on a kitchen table

when I had to be restrained & tube fed why did I want this? why did I not comply & try to get better?

three-car pileup, body kept from ricocheting around car by seatbelt

do I just crave intensity?

ID in a wallet

to what extent was I reacting to those boys when I was four?

loaf of bread in an oven

to what extent was I inventing an invisible friend because I was lonely?

girlchild in a well

to what extent did I want to shut all humans out, burn my forest?

father in a coffin

to what extent did I mistranslate everything I was told?

mother's voice on a phone, rapist's voice on a phone

to what extent was it simply ingrained habit: purging as quotidian as tooth-brushing?

panther pacing a cage

how does the desire to escape tie into being queer, e.g. being taught my basic perceptions & desires were wrong?

medical chart thick as my thigh in a dump

if bulimia taught me to be angry instead of passive, as in anorexia, was it a gift?

plastic bottles in a dump

if I had gone to prom or college instead of hospitals, if I'd had family or mentors, would I have become a queer poet?

           green beach glass washing ashore

if I had been functional enough to be in a relationship, might it have pulled me out?

           Ensure in a can

had I not been granted SSI / SSDI, would I have been capable of forcing enough stability for a job?

           napalm in a can

was my protracted convalescence simply simpering?

           empty cans clattering in the backseat: half Coors Lite, half Diet Coke

what if I don't know how great the scene was five years ago because I was too busy dying?

           empty gurney, empty shopping cart

am I using someone else's marginalization to demonstrate my own?

           shallow stitches in a teenage arm

is correlating the murder of a brown person with my white lived experience problematic to the point that this poem is irrevocably flawed?

           meal plan on a tray

a building can melt in enough heat, as from burning napalm, right?

           meal plan in the body

so why do freezing temperatures only create tiny fissures, at worst?

           ice in the marrow

what does a woman's body build & what does a man's body build?

           scraps I'd throw on the floor "accidentally"

how fine a lace have I knit my bones to & how early will I know?

           UNICEF rice on a helicopter shot down

what is the use of bricks?

           body thrown from Pinochet's helicopters into the ocean

what is the use of mulch, of peat?

                                                baby cut from corpse's stomach

why did I make a winter garden?

                                       ovaries shrunken grapes or swollen pears

why did I not stay in the winter palace?
kwashiorkor stomach
why is food used to describe a woman's body?

                           a house's shadow sliding slow across a lawn

why is architecture used to describe a man's?

                                      bone chips in a desert

does a decade of amenorrhea create visual changes to the appearance of the ovaries?

                                dimmest star in a constellation

what was I trying to say without using language?

                         the smallest white dwarfs collapse & are never named

to what extent was I using the master's tools or my own.

Shift Work

Top 40

There was a room where I was seen Woke up alone
in a body in which depth indicates

duration In El Paso dad died I worked
weddings The bartender lost two fingers Cuts in

the mountain across the border said the bible was
true / a well Kneeling, my reflection's logic was pinned

to self-assurance I'd seep away A father is a piano full
of bees Gender is a skirt of wet rocks Failing

to erode, I combed clouds to shreds hot enough to burn
a hole clean through my afternoon Each

afternoon A border's a slip, as in permission
or plummet or fissure or truth A body is

a hoodie left in a motel room a ball
of pink smoke a rush of brown water

closing over a thrown rock A mother is
why I cut the rotten part of my body off

and handed the rest to you Was left holding
a fistful of pebbles & no more dead lovers

besides you Sure I could have loved you
prettier The swerve of having survived

to go on telling your jokes worse To slouch in the RV
is to think of you thinking of duration I kept turning

away from tejano brushing my ankles like a mutt I forget
the point of pain with no lesson glued on Remember

the bartender's stubs had a wrinkled strip ·
like a tutu These sand-scrubbed places

blue light spools quartz-steady our days
drift into flyoverland Flat clumps hard to tell apart

Self-Portrait with Genetic Mutation

A place this insane,
          even the dogs hallucinate.
                    The babies' eyes
                              already blink hard as pebbles.
The dead just
          won't stay put where we bury them,
                    keep floating towards the rusty water.
                    My hair is sparking at the ends, trail
                              into the river: my family's thread
          of recklessness, begging
                    to get cut. When I think
          of money, I think of air

conditioners dripping
          on my shoulders, of being stranded
     in a subway car
               snarled under the river. Of my mother's tibia
     poking white through a red slick.
                              How the island was left
                    before the purple mangoes ripened.

Think of five miles to find
          clean water, of buying diet soda
                    at the corner. Ration
          cards and food stamp cards recharge inside

my people like diodes.
                    Walk home again to not pay
     the reduced-fare subway. Throw pennies in
          the water; throw nickels through

the stupid ghost swings
                    at the dead kids. Kept waiting
            for something else expensive
                to break, for my tibia to soften
                                    into cholla.

I think about my mother's hair
            growing longer. About running
                        it over my mouth.

Shift Work

I'm not sure how I decided
    to join the living but I know
        when it began: that winter so long
    persimmons lasted until April
        & the neighbors hissed until three a.m.

Pigeons flared in my rafters: a susurrus
    of oiled wings. Snow clung
        stubborn as shower scum.
    On the train we rocked
        as one, a catamaran pitch
    in green waves, a rocket
        toward where the exit would be.

I got better at taking the garbage out
        & making less. At the idea
    of getting better. The fridge hummed low to me
        with the wings. I kept
    a box of smoke & a fever under
        my bed. Blew on them before sleep,
        made a wish.

I thought of the jobs I thought I'd do.
    The job I did. Got up,
        went to work. Aligned my boots so
        careful on the platform.
    Ate the last persimmon.
        Went dark inside.

Under Pressure

Yes, I did know I was being used, & how. That's one
　　　of those songs someone's singing each second.
A seed-tray sprouts in the shed's darkest corner. Friday ten kids
　　　got shot. Tuesday a hurricane unshucked trees to matchsticks

two counties over. Just now I danced with a girl & when
　　　night breaks, she'll find another. I can't align with why I should hurt
my way up... nor why we ache to rely, & to believe for a moment
　　　time's malleable, & grows back green, & to forget hunger's tender

current. Slow star, quick blade. Night doesn't fall
　　　or break: it seeps like blood plumes in water—as silt,
as cream, as madness seeds wind. Books are a sheaf
　　　of corpses in the language of the victors. I'm to want to ink

my name on one in order to eke out my clearing. Houses are hollow
　　　reliquaries built from books. I'm sidling toward the door, a curtain
of 4/4 pulsing at my heels. I throw my career under a bus
　　　whenever possible, but I've never wanted to carve my love

into bark. Others have. Men on mountaintops blazed paths
　　　with their white names long after people palmed caves inside mountains
& blew red powder to show where they'd pressed. One removed;
　　　one accrued. Most of what I think about is how to get smaller

so there's more later. Good days, I'm frightened by this terrible tenderness
　　　tendriling in me: what's not discharged festers. Maybe I'm not cruel enough
to claw my way into the junkshop's interior, but I can't help dismantle the empire
　　　when I'm this stricken: knotting & unknotting my scarf, trailing my trauma

to the chip aisle again. I know this: bad nights, every angle's a wall & shadows blur
      but what seems set against us is only itself, breathing quiet. Listen. If trees could talk,
they wouldn't. That sigh isn't tree. It's wind. Driving, your oasis is heat: you'll have
      responses to this & the responses will have responders— the reams of ancestors

floating between us are who should be addressed. They can't be repaid. I've this long
      white debt. Various vistas will sweep around us, glow, get razed.
I should maybe go West for a bit. I'm sorry. The aftermath
      of destruction is predictably peculiar. A hurricane, for example: after a flood,

      fires start. One goes back. One's never done.

Lacuna

How to name an ache
A vestigial organ
a hollow
a tub of black water
forego the *the* of ache
of gone, pitching
caught crooked
our battles, suck out
is to know no
it is to have
jazz We learn by
silk The war
diesel into lake
silk and lake Thus
Our gendered
smooth spasm or psalm
I'm in now but
human & I choke
my hands are tender
was I'm always meat
banks affix
meaning to a life A body

that no longer snags
pulled out leaves
Reasons open into
On the bus we pretend we'll
The lacuna Street thick black
vinyl's heavy hiss Needle
on a lush wheel Let's pick
the splinters To be poor
alternative to pulled backs To know what
no alternative Without blues, no
unforgetting, press whats into
of caring, roar of green
An object cannot be both
a person cannot be both
sputtering palms
I forget which now
in the tub we are post
water from my eyes Because
He assumed my intention
or money Blood
to dollar stores Posthumously we affix

flashes A body floats
in its mosses Perhaps posthumously
a body is a forgetting Perhaps forgetting opens
a door gone holy & by entering we wrest
out proximal redemption The brass general
glares into the park His horse looks frightened Our ball

                         keeps turning slowly I'll meet you wherever
the *there* is When the incident
                         replaces the projected When the projection
replaces the actual On the bus
                         grief's incidental On the bus I'm sure
                                   it's not too late to leave

The Game

before the seizures & the winter
       had taken their cut, that bad hunger blew in
with dirt in her teeth, the old ex's pull
       undertowing the town from within,
waves we could magic like fanning
       air, gods we could wed or topple
with sticky notes, rules for getting good
       & what good was & a road there, waves
of stars in her hair, belief rolling in easy as
       the girl who figured them all out, who refused
the breadcrumbforest, who taught herself to fish
       in the dark with a candle how the wardens
say not to, waves of grass squashing
       under hooves, hunger's marled teeth gnashing back,

back, explained as vanity over-controlled, never
       in the pamphlets as the wish to be consumed
          by becoming consumed with consumption,
       not a convulsive reaction to the glut, a refusal
to adhere, "girl" as trapdoor jumped through & shut,
       as wreckage after Pandora's box opened,
          as branches strewn over the road, the one to blame
       for that apple / rib thing, as a false way to cinch time's
coruscating ribbon, key to the doorknob into the storm
       turning, storm we'd walk into with
          no rope, the storm's dream of the attics's heart,
       the eaves a bed to hide under from the storm,
the storm wanting to take in order to break so no one else
            could ruin & the cattails waving, then flattened, & the girl
dreaming of walking with the storm, & the times they
       wouldn't let her walk, wheeled her around, wouldn't believe

or let her explain, got degrees to teach her the rules she
must've forgotten, surely, & the storm now dreaming of waves
of damp grass parting under feet as men say water can
with a man's hand, & the press a body makes in grass
when it has gone, the storm dreaming of seeing her walk
down the tiled hallway wheeling her machine & the storm turning
its face away, saddened, falling back into dreams the logic of
the recurring tawdry dream one can't stop falling into,
rough-charcoaled study of the "girl" who threw
up a whole hallway, threw up her weight every day,
the other "girl" too small to activate automatic doors, the deer
that bounds off when close enough to touch, dream fun-house
angles, high-school art of a candle melted
onto a box, the title bad, *The Storm's Dream*,
Girl As Forest Fire, a predictable jump
shot, cheap cut, punch in the gut, rough water
& bread, peasant hands, rotten fish, murky light, teacher fishing
for the name of a painter too minor to recall, hands purposely
hidden so as not to have to render, fat rendering, horizons collapsed,
"girl's" perspective too "narrow," the wrong box checked,
gift unopened, letter returned, expired box
of meat, grocer's shelves ransacked before the storm,
teacher's predictions over-inflated, certain dangers
disregarded, nothing to lose, windows taped with X, man
on his porch with a shotgun, tallymark for body numbers
or for places to sleep, cartoon eyes crossed with X for love

or for death, the illiterates' signature, her signature move—
generating trash, xxxxxo—then the movement's dispersal,
waves of communication guttering out

as the relationship floats South, useless emergency
candle box, gun that doesn't go off, power wasted
by the powerless due to the uselessness of power, time
wasted on fear because of uselessness & guilt, fire
alarm brat-pulled, tacky cinematic threat to jump
off a ledge so the man can rescue, plot device to bolster
his heroism, not about her, not the actual act of plunging into a lake,
the questions about the likelihood of jumping, internal question
of violation vs. disclosure, narcissism in wanting to keep
the likelihood secret but wanting the question, those years
likely-to-die, thinking the choice to live edge-floating

through imperialism could be a protest against imperialism,
a non-binary non-response to the question of living, lake-light
murky with drink, the desperate choice, the "girl" fallen
from the back of a truck, the stowaway, the magician's
sword not slicing the girl, "girl" not jumping out of a cake, carnival
weight guessed incorrectly, the rictus needle trembling, the fall's
impact measured & bones set, recovery explained
as moment of diagnosis, bodies a tunnel scratched out,
nurse checking the beds to make sure the "girls" are breathing,
warden's flashlight sweeping the false feet, tunnel sealed, the opening
in the stomach for the feed, brainstem for shunt, tremor giving
the problem away, after lobotomies they'd induce seizures,
just to check, the girl given away by her father,
the weatherman's greasy gesture at his green-screen,

radar sweep, hurricane's eye, tree rings giving away
the drought years when rations ran low, bones sucked
to lace, floodwaters receding, shucked corn, famine explained
in terms of the rescue party's arrival, waves of evacuation,

women & children first, not how they'd survived while lost,
the flood-line's stain, her water breaking, her refusal to bleed,
we've got the story backwards, hip breaks *before* fall,
lightning comes *up* from the ground, glass-fries sand, radio dial

churns through static, *looks* for noise, not creates, queerness & passing
both attempts to code-switch off the grid of conventional attraction
for safety, not "becoming attractive" "taken too far,"
the magpie's wheel, the man's one-knee kneel
one time only, the wedding ring's glint in the drain,
magpie looking through the chimney for metal,

blue ring of gas on the stove, the foolish need to check,
steering wheel in junked car in the river, body
under ice, chemical murk, frozen smoke, windows soaped,
the new name impossible to learn, non-gender
foolish as the dog under the bed from a storm, the wolf

in a trap chewing its leg off, & wheelchair on a beach
stuck in sand, the girl's both-knee kneel, mouth moving,
not speaking, & would you believe I'm not the "girl"
& the dream someone else recounted & the story
she wants to reel back once told & the fishbone
in her throat & the dark funnel & the well
& the sobbing over apples & the floating edge never
happened, would not happen again, never, she knows
now, this was before their white noise got into our entrails, before

we were saved, broke up, before the storm broke
like an ankle & dawn washed in orange & the audience

began to clap, before the fever broke as soap breaks oil,
before the storm's dream hung meat for the winter,
or the "girl's" friend's mother got the box with the other girl's ashes,
which does not mean the friend won, before the storm
got big enough to be named a girl's name & the people
learned how to make soap from ashes & fat & the stadium
collapsed & was rebranded & the termites tunneled
in again & the storm woke up with its pillow wet.
tattered platitudes wheel through their woodwork.
that bad ex is so tempting, but it won't work.
there are rules. they want our good girl skin.

Don't Speak Ill

I feed my dead enemies mud and suitcases. I build them an attic,
a kiva, a view through the keyhole to our feast. I throw
open my windows to let their wind in; I weave them
a ladder to hunger. The ladder's a noose, and a failure.
When they're sad, I climb it and snuff out the moon for them.
I crush my hunger into a diode to feed my dead enemies.
I spit out a totem and a token for them. I make them a mix tape
but they can't play it because nobody has a tape player anymore,
not even the dead. I make them a Spotify playlist
but I delete it after I send the email, embarrassed
because it's cheesy. I promise a concert instead. I sing a song
for every cheese I've ever eaten, and when they fall
asleep, bored, I tuck the blanket tighter around my dead enemies
like cellophane over my face and mutter bitterly about
the fatal flaw in every therapist's theory of me. When they
wake up, sloe-eyed, I name every friend I'll never see again.
I knit them a shawl for the colder winters, a fishnet
to catch night, a chain link fence so they can press
cunning diamonds into their skins to match the shawl. I embroider
them with, varyingly, a smokestack, a smoker,
the smoker's jaw. I lovingly codex each calamity to catch them up: rich men
and their dirty money, men and their guns, poor men and their rich
food, white men and their gutting of poor
villages for slaves or pretty lakes, women and their lakes
of feelings, poor women and their bad tattoos, the lake
the size of an envelope, the envelope the size of a pocket
mirror, the overdue bill envelope, the tattoo of a fan, a silhouette,
the tattooed girl flapping on the mudflap, the girlchild with a sheaf
of temporary Ariel tattoos. I walk through the woods petting boulders
for my dead enemies. I walk through the city stealing

incense. I feed them hyssop, hominy, my tattoos,
and how they'll look on me at 80. It is summer,
it is winter, and the pages turn in wind. I think
they were almost happy here. When I want to touch
my dead enemies, I wrap my arms closer around my elbows.

Service Industry

For G., K., & L.

Rich boys wait for me to pour; I wait til
I can flip their chairs & sit. My dead friends all

have hands like horses & perfect teeth
now. The bus partway-home screams

by. I'm not getting on. Most of our lives, some camera's
recording. Nobody will watch. Some star implodes.

I Paypal flower money for the latest hearse
on my phone. Cellophane tap first cigarette out, flip,

ease back in. The last I'll smoke.
In this pack. A lightning-struck tree stops

smoldering. I pour their beers. Sneak a shot.

If her drowning was a declaration,
the message was muddled but kept pouring

into all hollows, skin or soil, sunk in
quick. When I wake, it's still raining

& I don't have much to say. Skim-milk sun. Wet
starlings & butts huddled on my sill. Seventeen

emails. Downstairs under the tree, a kid coughs or laughs.

We were glazed with sickness. Til we left.
Between groups we'd glide down the hall, blankets

spun to capes. Dinners, I'd step off
with a nurse. Of course I'd radiate her pain back

on me. Really, it wasn't a drowning. Her heart stopped.
In her sleep. Of course you'd want to know

how she died, & why.

Mansion, Apartment, Shack, House

Whether time got away from me or
caught up with me is hard to say,
        the shape of its shadow is the same.
Rupture in the silhouette of a house.
        The house was the beginning
of a puddle of milk, forest
        before the fire, before our nostrils blackened
with ash. Houses break lawns
        like shadows. I've taken to pretending
there's a thumb pressing the bad
        spot in my skull, tamping the fever. Trepan,
a compass needling not-quite-north.
        The city air's stippled plaid. I move my sour
face around it, waver
        in doorways. Flicker scraps
of fryer, laundromat. I've taken to shoving men aside
        to order at bars. I've given up
asking what I can do to help. I've taken to
        doing. Suffer the flames
but not what started the fire. Sure I don't eat
        in public, but I plug in the
banter until brittle, until I can walk back to the room
        where papered lamplight spills gentle over my mess.
Suffer the mess. Air breaks sticks like deer. Wind breaks bodies
        like men. We do the most we can. Desert towns
break teeth & horses faster. Born with
        with lungs that didn't open like flowers but
like sickles. Heartland towns rust out fastest,

point and shoot, factory soot. Born in a
hospital room where twenty-seven people
        died. Cities break buildings faster. One collapses
each spring, just as the geese
        start to come home. I've given up thinking
anything is the most I can do.
        I'm not broken. Air parts around my walking
like a prow. Moreover, I'm not inscrutable
        I'm frightened. For
us all. Suffer the fear. Do not call me
        darling if you're higher. I refuse
to be reforested. I stay razed
        as a reminder. I know words
are mostly transactions,
        but they taste like flint.

The Detritus Eaters

Good friends a raft   of smoke, a proxy gender. Our good
     debt what it is   to leak
  a sheet of frost,   to be their sponge.
  Our family tree   in caution
          tape. Our fathers' debt and what
    it is to be who   has been sloughed, what cleans up.
Are we burnish   or scour? We forgot they wouldn't
  let them die   how a god dies. We foxed under
          their current.   Brambles
          they know us.   Our ripped
          pockets.   There are
       a thousand tiny winks.   A city's
       far off shining   ʼ   like the cufflinks
    of the disposably incomed   but babe
       it's not for us.   That's for what our
    brothers muddled   and all that
    keening afterward.   Lie down.
Here's where our   queer shoulders touch.
 Ten thousand points of   manifestos
lurching languid yet the   census men they make
no box for us to check.   Why does not getting
       killed matter   so much
          to me? Lie down lie
  down lie down.   Wet leaves
  will dry or rot.   A tree's a sentence
broken at the root.   No gate. A crocus bulb's a mouth

          of ash.   What do I have
       to say about   violence. I swipe
       my card.   I'll never have
    a kid. Iron filings   silt the borough.
    Such hopeful   names the streets have in that city:

Occlusions. Useless flowers like

rhododendrons.   Wednesday the townspeople

          make lace   of extension

          cords.   Thursday's a handful of hollow

     point bullets   tossed on the coffin. Today's

spring cleaning. Red days   we can always make

               an us.   We make a syntax

     for our kitchen.   We burn it. Darlings,

          you don't have   to be afraid,

               but you probably should be.

Self-Portrait with Junk Bonds & Accordion

When I returned to the palace
The fountains were full
Of leaves & they said
I still wasn't
Welcome no more. Pieces of
Me I starved broke
Away and made
Their own mistakes. I burn
My cash for good
Luck. The pears in
Our teeth. The pear
Tree's glut a cluster of
Planets. I burned
The orchard so I
Could mend the fence between
The years I stole
Away and the wrist
She broke. I dug them posts
For the down
Payment so men
In white could cut
A window at the place
In her hand where afternoon slips
Her tongue to night. Sunsets,
I rip bits from webs of
Minor gods & feed them
To the war's traffic
In clean bones. My tariff a handful
Of salt. Her fingers a tangle
Of copper wire. Her copper hair
A finger scratching through a map,

Ripping open a credit report.
One way I can explain
My country is to say my people
Came over to bring
Your people over in chains to build
The palace I was brought into
In chains & I'm sorry
Doesn't help. I've this white debt
The palace didn't
Help. We're no good
At being helpful. One way I can
Explain what I did
In the palace is some
Years fall into bad
Habits & later the habits fall
Into disrepair.
He won't listen
To me say one
Way I can explain
My country is a labyrinth
With a night
Market in it. He'll order
A dead bird for me. In one stall
In the night market there's
A city made of
Popsicle sticks & a
Minotaur made of teeth &
Grease & it's us.
If you look at it from above
We're on this shining grid
& we land & remember

It's a cage but how
Gold that latticework. Each point
Where two bars meet
Is a constellation,
A back door blooming open
Like a bomb. My city
Is a backyard full of blackening
Petals. This riot is not
A fable or a metaphor. I am telling
You the truth. I am telling
You everything. I'm making
A face under my face. Any body
That looks like a girl's a fence &
Behind it's a wall
Of flames. Darlings, let's drive
Until the highway ends at an
Ocean & on the beach a
Franchised palace where girls
Dragged in sob & shove
Their plates away.
Each city's summer
Will husk into the
Sweet rot of what
They thought we'd
Be the night
With the crown of
Black plastic feathers. The silken
Hand of the East
River's reaching
Up for us. I'm sucking down
My last drag. Done

Wanting what they
Wanted for me. Thick
Squalls extinguish our insipid
Sun. Spill over the
Levee. They'll take us
Down to the ward
To be raked over. I'm sorry
I swear I can still
Hear the trees
Humming.
They're hungry.

100 Works in Mill Aluminum

It was weather when you and who met.
You looked at culture and agreed difficulty.
It was set somewhere blurry-Western.
It was a volatile production.
It was a healthy injection.
It was a lengthy sensation.
It had a commanding presence.
Race, sexuality, class, and gender were not entirely unconsidered, but.
The incongruity was the humorous part.
The spontaneity kept it nimble.
A menu is sticky.
There was a generational disparity.
You and who purchase calories.
You consume them in proximal semi-public.
Who says it does not connote. The curation lags.
The aesthetic is of a mismanaged quorum.
You suggest intentional awkward heightening, then feel awkward.
You inquire on the progress of who's life event. You agree the difficulty has
usefully clarified your relational emotions.
Though as always it is hard to look at how close we are, societally, to an end.
Separation and transport occur.
Mid-liminality you're reviewing your dumbest moments.
Until you pass a tree full of wind chimes.
A block after you pass a tree full of lights.
Each produces an identical emotion.
Due to a reaction in your anterior insula.
In part *because* it is night. You have
at least three other senses. Perhaps more—
dimensions vary. Gross streets are empty
inside you. People miss their dead. They shove new

plastic bags into their bag of bags. You're beyond
changing. Yours is a country with a greedy
luminosity that wears out its lovers. A settee
beckons. Be somebody with a body. You squish
tick into smear. You pave a bumpy road
via fro-yo spoon. You send a wind chime out
invisibly. You do not deny anything.
Nothing recurs.

Stop—You Were Never Gonna Get to Live on Their Farm / Plantation; When They Die Their Fascist Scion'll Take Over

When the phoenix is reborn the land has changed,
but the phoenix is the same. Loud. I guess we always start

with fear: by the lake my mother sent me an umbrella, a stolen
sunset. It's always been too late. I've never been as good as glass, but I know

where the cracks are. I drink my drink. I try. I pick my nails,
a lucky number. S., hold my arm. I've been not touched bad

wire. O no, much sun touches me & I consider my emergency
contacts: shells in the trundle bed, shot fixed on night

stand, stand up, wake & forget, half & half white, white. I try
on child labor cottons, layer static. Let's bask in crushed styrofoam until sun's

a seam to rip yellowed teeth through. No white man has no hold
on me. I'd be lying if I said I believed in sunsets

or that my face in the glass-bottom wasn't becoming
darker. The boat's hold fixed me lying. My fingers wanted to braid

A.'s hair. I sat on them. I mean I'm afraid
to connect because I'm afraid to impose. I sat on hold

all morning. I've stopped pretending I know about umbrellas
or collapse. I've never been but I found F. where it ends:

with fear. Needles always moves north & my veins
always roll. Let's build a ritual from the ashes of old

ways to not freak out. I swarm out, leave dresses
collapsed. I can't fix this. No, I'm not scared I'm a light growing big

in a tunnel. I mean I'm not scared it's over so I climb the stairs
onto the ocean floor. When those girls lived still, shooting,

shot I'd find them fists, curled there. Now, I put
my bread where it can soak into the blood, tongue sawdust.

It's good to pray on how what was built for us
by the dead was built by grifting hands.

Take Your Places, Ladies

I take my fear for a walk around the neighborhood / before the thunderhead
rolls down. Rip the silk / of night from night, wrap the silk around a coin

with the face of the king / for cream in morning. / You float / dahlias in water,
fill the arms / of the yard / with orange blossoms and static.
My face is this object / I carry around everywhere I go

and I'm starting to not mind this. / How much of me is not
a man. / How weak is any part of a woman

trying to speak. I hold a candle safely / in my body.
I hold a rainstorm / safely in my mouth. / Too often, when I finish
eating, I'm sad because I can't keep eating. I have / this thing called agency. You have

this thing called privilege. We both know / which king's checked and which of us
is a rook. Your birdsong / and geography are meaningless. Empty

the dish drain for once. I mean road / when I say pray. I mean road
when I say window. I mean you / when I say road. What shape
does a year make? What skin does a / year change? How perfect his white

hands were in the dream. / I sleep the deepest with
his hair growing over my throat. / You have come down from
the kingdom on the mountain / to tell us something / very important. I'm stirring

the sauce for your dinner. I'm remembering how / the train track curved
at a latitude. Just right to / smash quarters. I cook a rabbit /

and a nest of hair. / Trace the latitude / of wind into the king's palm. Slide
a rusting coin under his tongue. / I drive my fear south to your door.
I stand on your porch with an open mouth / as if about to speak.

Murmur in the Inventory

Glass bottle on platform. Stain blot / from carpet.
I tell you I'm not hungry / but that's the wrong question.
It's whether I'll / eat. Some mornings looking
out the window as grapefruit / light unspools
through the glass / tumbler of our living

room, my mouth waters. / Her living corpse a cicada shell
held under my tongue all morning. / Days chug on & they're
lovely & I'm tired / of light & more tired of light we make when the sun's gone
to bed. Some faces open / as the hand in the dream
where their bodies rose / out of the lake, got dressed again, before
the sedan drove back up / onto the bridge. I tell you my war's

over. We both know / I'm lying. We're born & die in various rooms,
some a series of tiny punctures, some a / suture, some a bead
on a string, a lozenge. / She could smell the moment
bread was ready. Whoever / you almost-died with once
hasn't become a tree. A lot / could still
happen, couldn't it? / C'mon, remind me height's the same
as fingertip to fingertip, how / this suggests wingspan. There's a pond

in your iris / quickening, oil-thick crabapple sky
you fell into. / In me, a handful / of salt. Some girls are born accidents.
Some accidents blow south, semis / carrying cattle, carrying
oil. I'm looking / to fall into / some trouble. Forget how to fold
a sweater, a hand. Fold like a card. / Some almost-die together
& apart later & sometimes the accident / is on purpose.

It's not the light, / it's what it hits, open or close

fisted. Not the lilacs but the dust / on them, the water they drink. Dust
is mostly skin. The day recalled / backwards & the dream
forwards & the death a / second, a stutter. I'm having a hard time

sleeping. I wanted a long

polished corridor we'd walk down,

clipping our purposeful heels. Our shoes ice

cream green in summer,

burnished leather in winter,

imported all year round.

What happened was in the forest there was

a deerpath I thought

I heard her further on.

I was barefoot, one toe cut, no

magnolia in my hair but they seemed

to fill my throat. What my uncle did

& her father did   were not accidents. I sit at a desk
& move my hands the way   I memorized before we knew knowing
would be imperative. I fix   them to put out fires, unstitch mold

from bread, pad the nest   with dirty laundry. I spent years
being asked to describe   my feelings & for the record I'm not angry
but maybe I should try it.   By which I mean what is
the right question? It's not   whether we're contaminated
it's the type of poison &   what this says about us.
Taste is a weapon of class,   sure, but I'm not sick
of the world or sitting in it   sharing a cheap bottle with you.
I'm not sick anymore   but   I'm sickened, so when the sun
snuffs itself out I go   swimming. There'll never be a photograph
of the years we broke like   sticks but we could burn them,
cook a creature's tiny limbs   over the fire, eat it.
Years I woke up   & walked through with my tiny
legs cramping.   Stick your   arms in the wind.

I'm having a hard time being awake.

What happened was I saw her walking past my door on a Tuesday. She died on a Friday.

My toes curled in purple jelly shoes, $8 on the street.

Her hair the flag of a gone country.

What happened is I didn't know. Then I did.

Everyone still kept talking about what a beautiful day.

And it was: dust motes glinting slanted, a bowl of lilacs floating in water.

(I didn't
        grow the lilacs myself, but she would've
                liked them. I didn't cut them down

but I watched them circle in the bowl, watched
my face change in the water. My watching
didn't keep them from browning.
My body hungry. My body eating.
My body's fickle childish
factory: pumping out plastic
bags to fill the forest, churning
out mud to dirty
our corridor.)
(What I did to my temples, my collarbones
was a furious fixing. A way to undaughter. Our lady
of pitiful disclosures & pitying looks
back at the pillar.)

Suffer the dust & all the fathers & uncles gone,
sweet curls their bodies make under the white oak.
What I did a grift, a graft. A bedroom can be a raft
or a cliff. Year a fever, day
a silo. Voice the heat of a plane landing. Lungs Dixie cups
of gasoline for the wrong
girl to fill. A spark thrown. Her dead face
a blue square. Her face a cartoon
or a sunset. Sure, I'm haunted, but the ghosts
are finger-oil glossing the same spot
on a screen. My face
in strangers' hands. My heavy-trafficked face.
My ctrl + f hands. A girl with a voice like a public
bathroom lock. A girl made
of a blinking cursor. From this off far light
years are tiny. Nights,
I swipe the moon across the sky.

My drink across the room.

                Walk away from me. Go the direction

the pine needles point.

              They'll take you back.

They're mumbling a prayer

              but it's not for us.

It's to warn the others about us:

              our lousy habit

of making windows,

              then making steam,

years of paper

              no one will read. I am scratching

on a corpse.

              With my pen.

What happened is she's not dead. She's a walking IV pole. / She's not dead but I / could have gone where she is. / I say I'm going away instead. I'm not sure / it's better. / We thought death would be a graceful slide / princess on a barge / hair blooming underwater / her red mouth a door / her mouth on fire / too thin to break snow / slow fade in Victorian nightgown. / It's not. / Then there's my dad / ghosting around the edges. / What good is it to witness pain / protracted & unresolvable / until death, which is not a resolution? / I'm using her sad life / to write a sad poem / about myself. / I can't think about her/ without reducing her to her body / I can't write about her body / without using words like ash or bird or paper. She's not dead / but when she dies everyone will still / keep saying what a nice day it is if it is / & some teenagers / will make a memorial page / with sparkly before-&-after after .gifs. / Another one of us will be next. / I am complicit. / My bones are lace. / I don't bleed. I refuse to bleed. / My dad's disease might be in me. / Stuff a mouth with chrysanthemums.

What happened was it wasn't my
                father or my uncle. What happened was
        I don't remember what happened
in the woodshed or how many
                boys there were. I know that year, my
        haircut was snipped around a blue cereal bowl.
        My collarbones are still there, just a little.
                        The shorn nape of my neck is not a request.
                        It's a dare.

In the dream, she's running on two broken ankles.

In Minneapolis this morning, she's on the elliptical with two sprained ankles.

I have been complicit. When she saw me first she started crying.

Wouldn't talk to me until I was a few meals in.

I say I'm better, but I haven't eaten a meal with anyone in two months.

I'm making this about me again. I'm sorry. I love the world. I do.

I say too much because I was taught poking at the dark would save me. It didn't.

My pain isn't unique or worse; I don't want to sit in it. But: I can't go to brunch without it
sitting splayed between us.

My friend holds her child & rocks. Sprinkle salt   under my tongue. What language
do you dream in? I'm pushing for   good & I'm pushing my tongue against
the roof of my mouth as I grin for the camera.   My death waiting
in my jawbone. What do I know   about refuge. What it is to be

a problem. The one who has   a problem. Girl as a handful
of numbers measuring the girl.   Sky as a handful of salt. First name basis
with two phlebotomists.   What incurable means to the mountains. How my t-shirt smells
after the mountains. When the kings   wanted to know the weight of smoke
they burned the cigar and measured ash.   By which I have these hours, body
emptied & filled, charts spilling thick as a girl-thigh.   Paper is a corpse.
I'm crushing in the corners   of the box. Who the mountain spat out
Walk on the safe side of the street   (less bushes)
through two stages of grief to brunch.   Cut a grapefruit fancy.
Mackerel isn't just a sky. Lungs   aren't only a bellows. I've named your power
uit. Brunch is a feminist issue. Aggressive   Instagram the bloody
Mary; scroll past skeletons. Every teacup   its own curl of steam. Every personal
tragedy political. Gut-rot   isn't just what happened
to the man who ran the fruit-stand.   Before the bank took the farm. Thick smoke
blows in the screen door from the   archipelago, laddering out the tired-trotted
hum of that burned decade. The   islands keep changing position
as night gutters out across the ceiling.   We're trying very hard to break
the horses before spring turns   its back on us. The day recalled backwards as
death occurs backwards: grapefruit   light unspools, the sedan drives back
out, coated in pondweed. My mouth waters.   There's air in my cupboards I could fill.

(Look: there's a little flare
in each of us down a well. I can push
whatever I want in or out of the well
but I can't change the flare.)

Here's where I say something
comforting so you can go home
without feeling sad. Again. There's pink light
on the mountains. Some days are meant to
be hollow— that's how beads get strung. Bright scraps
of trash we were born of & bear & bare. Some girls
want to stay missing.
I keep waking up

126

before she hits the ground.
Some years get stuck between stations:
a radio, a subway. Tell me even the heaviest
metal can move. Something about god & a rock.
How light keeps expanding
& we don't know where it ends.
Spit out the chrysanthemums. Eat light.
Eat a sandwich. Darlings, I'm not writing this
with you in mind
but you're there.

Photo: Rijard Bergeron

Nina Puro's writing is in *Guernica*, the *PEN / America Poetry Series*, *Witness*, & others, including chapbooks from Argos Books and dancing girl press. They are a member of the Belladonna* Collaborative and recipient of fellowships from the MacDowell Colony, Syracuse University (MFA, 2012), Deming Fund, & others.

Nina is a social worker in Brooklyn, NY.

The New Issues Poetry Prize

Nina Puro, *Each Tree Could Hold a Noose or a House*
2017 Judge: David Rivard

Courtney Kampa, *Our Lady of Not Asking Why*
2016 Judge: Mary Szybist

Sawnie Morris, *Her, Infinite*
2015 Judge: Major Jackson

Abdul Ali, *Trouble Sleeping*
2014 Judge: Fanny Howe

Kerrin McCadden, *Landscape with Plywood Silhouettes*
2013 Judge: David St. John

Marni Ludgwig, *Pinwheel*
2012 Judge: Jean Valentine

Andrew Allport, *the body | of space | in the shape of the human*
2011 Judge: David Wojahn

Jeff Hoffman, *Journal of American Foreign Policy*
2010 Judge: Linda Gregerson

Judy Halebsky, *Sky=Empty*
2009 Judge: Marvin Bell

Justin Marks, *A Million in Prizes*
2008 Judge: Carl Phillips

Sandra Beasley, *Theories of Falling*
2007 Judge: Marie Howe

Jason Bredle, *Standing in Line for the Beast*
2006 Judge: Barbara Hamby

Katie Peterson, *This One Tree*
2005 Judge: William Olsen

Kevin Boyle, *A Home for Wayward Girls*
2004 Judge: Rodney Jones

Matthew Thorburn, *Subject to Change*
2003 Judge: Brenda Hillman

Paul Guest, *The Resurrection of the Body and the Ruin of the World*
2002 Judge: Campbell McGrath

Sarah Mangold, *Household Mechanics*
2001 Judge: C.D. Wright

Elizabeth Powell, *The Republic of Self*
2000 Judge: C.K. Williams

Joy Manesiotis, *They Sing to Her Bones*
1999 Judge: Marianne Boruch

Malena Mörling, *Ocean Avenue*
1998 Judge: Philip Levine

Marsha de la O, *Black Hope*
1997 Judge: Chase Twichell